CROSSWORDS
FOR
KIDS

VOLUME TWO

by
Dr. Linda Lawrence

Edited by
Will Reardon

Cover by
Tracy Downs

Copyright 2004 by Linda Lawrence. Printed in the U.S.   ISBN 0-9716039-1-X

YOU CAN DO IT!

Answers to the puzzles are found at the back of the book. The page number of the puzzle is the puzzle number for the answers.

IT IS
NOT
CHEATING

TO USE THE
ANSWERS!

Just try to do the puzzle by yourself first. Then use the answers to help you finish. You will automatically learn new words each time and then you'll be an

EXPERT!

SIX STEPS TO SUCCESS

1. BE SURE YOU KNOW THE WORDS IN THE WORD LIST.

2. USE A PENCIL, NOT A PEN

3. FILL IN ALL THE **ACROSS** WORDS THAT YOU KNOW AND SKIP THE ONES YOU DON'T KNOW.

4. THEN FILL IN ALL THE **DOWN** WORDS YOU KNOW, SKIPPING THE ONES YOU DON'T KNOW.

5. NOW SKIP AROUND AND TRY TO FILL IN THE REST OF THE WORDS.

6. GO TO THE ANSWERS IF YOU GET STUCK.

SPECIAL HINTS

1. If you only know the end of the word, just put it in first. (If it is plural, just put the "S" in the last box of the word)
2. PRE means before.
3. A PREFIX is a letter or letters at the front of a word that changes the meaning.
4. A SUFFIX is letters that come at the end of a word to change the meaning.
5. EST are letters at the end of a word meaning the MOST.
6. RE at the beginning of a word means "OVER AGAIN."
7. Sometimes part of a phrase is used.
   (Tra, La, _____) The answer is LA.
   (Wizard of ____) The answer is OZ.
8. Sometimes word games are used.
   (Middle of the BOAT) the answer is OA.

ABOUT THE TIME

THERE ARE DIFFERENT WAYS OF WRITING THE NAMES OF CENTURIES

Many people use B.C. to indicate the centuries before the time of Christ and A.D. to indicate the centuries after Christ. Many people in the world are not Christians and have trouble with this system. As a result, scientists use a scientific method that everyone in the world can understand, regardless of religion

THE SCIENTIFIC METHOD

The times we live in now are referred to as
The COMMON ERA or C.E.
The olden times are referred to as
BEFORE THE COMMON ERA or B.C.E.
Just as you need to know about metric measure and standard measure, you need to be familiar with these terms, too.

A QUEST IS A SEARCH

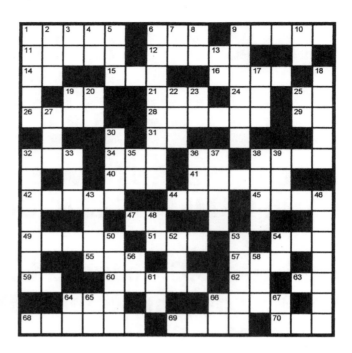

ACROSS

1. Opposite of BELOW
6. Plus; in addition to
9. _____ in Wonderland
11. Jewish clergyman
12. Having to do with the moon
14. Egyptian sun god
15. A short sleep
16. A small ship
19. Opposite of AND
21. Finished bottom of material
24. Prefix meaning NOT
25. In the morning; before noon
26. Tell of impending danger
28. Approximately; the path of a circle
29. Stands for ADVANCED PLACEMENT
31. Ammo for an air rifle
32. You have one on each side
34. Consumed
36. First two letters of the alphabet
38. Has ability; can do

40. A way to make lace
41. A girl's name
42. Cities
44. Automobile
45. A plant in the shape of something
47. Opposite of FROM
49. A search, sometimes for a treasure
51. Say a question
54. A donkey
55. A cheap metal
57. Contraction for IT IS
59. Abbreviation for EUROPEAN UNION
60. It carries blood
62. An American soldier
63. Opposite of STOP
64. Black goo that's used to seal things
66. What you think with; obey
68. A dog, a cat, a horse...
69. Kind of chemical; sour; tart
70. Opposite of OR

DOWN

1. You shoot it with a bow
2. What a sheep says
3. One who delivers babies
4. Abbreviation for VERB
5. ONE in Germany
6. Letters used to make words
7. First letters of NUMB
8. Abbrev. for DOWN
9. Same as 28 ACROSS
10. Colorado
13. First two letters of the alphabet
17. Same as 6 ACROSS
18. Enough
19. Partner of EITHER
20. A nurse's degree
22. Last letters in HERB
23. Slang for MORE
25. Size of a battery
27. Beg. of ACROSS
29. Beginning of apple
30. Blind night flyers
32. Very old
33. Cut grass
35. Half of an English good-bye
36. As in "with ice cream"
37. Old-fashioned word for POET
38. Part of your foot
39. "_____, humbug!"
43. A bird's house
46. Run away with stolen goods
48. Middle of BOAT
50. A lacy crown of jewels for women
52. Opposite of STAND
53. Stiff; unbending;
54. Big ___ a house
56. Opposite of YES
58. A cheap metal
61. Abbreviation for ROUTE
64. The leaf of a tea plant
65. Exist
66. Do, Re, __ __
67. District Attorney

WORDS

AA	ERB
AB	EU
ABLE	GI
ABOVE	GO
ABSCOND	HEM
ACID	ITS
ACR	LAURA
A LA	LUNAR
ALICE	MI
ALPHABET	MIND
AM	MO
A.M.	MOW
AMPLE	NAP
AND	NEST
ANIMAL	NO
ANTIQUE	NU
AORTA	OA
AP	OB
ARCH	OR
ARM	QUEST
AROUND	RA
ARROW	RABBI
AS	RIGID
ASK	RN
ASS	RT
ATE	SIT
BAA	TA
BAH	TAR
BARD	TAT
BATS	TI
BB	TIARA
BOAT	TIN
CAR	TO
CHIA	TOWNS
CO	UN
DA	VB
DN	WARN
EIN	

WHERE IS IT?

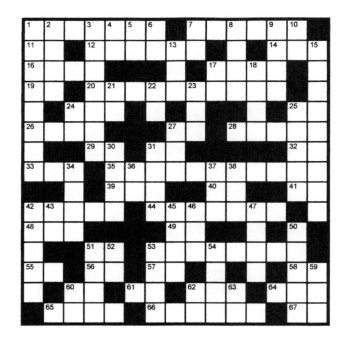

ACROSS

1. The only state with a "Z" in its name
7. Las Vegas is its capital
11. Prefix meaning AGAIN
12. It takes 12 to make a foot
14. Small stinging insect
16. Retain ownership
17. A kind of candy; where money is made
19. Short for ALFRED
20. State with a Pacific beach
24. Opposite of DAUGHTER
25. Like THE
26. Spoken
27. All right
28. A metric measurement in England
29. Letter after "el"
31. Over, upon
32. Stands for GOVERNMENT SERVICE
33. A bad or evil deed
35. Daring

39. Female deer
40. From
41. Letter after "Dee"
42. A northeastern state famous for lobsters
44. Its capitol is Albany
48. Feel sick
49. Short for WASHINGTON
51. Not yes
53. A southern state where a famous horse race is held
55. Northeast
56. Open wide and say "____"
57. Exists
58. THE in Spanish and Italian
60. The Wizard of _____
61. Air Conditioning
62. Wet dirt
64. Opposite of AGAINST
65. A Midwestern state
66. Another Midwestern state
67. New Mexico

8

DOWN

1. Pres. Clinton was from this state
2. A fishing rod has one; a dance
3. Every state has one
4. Over; above
5. North Carolina
6. Sound of contentment
7. Initials for Nancy Smith
8. Self-absorbed; boastful; overly proud
9. Information for use
10. First two letters of ANOTHER
13. One of Santa's helpers
15. Nashville is its capital
17. Master: abbrev.
18. Opposite of UNKIND
21. Beginning of ANOTHER
22. Nine in old Rome
23. An acorn becomes one
24. YES in Spanish and Italian
25. Disagree during a discussion
27. The first number
30. Created
31. Where to bake a pie
34. Usually goes with a hammer
36. Act
37. Plaything
38. Unidentified Flying Object
42. Same as 42 ACROSS
43. Two vowels
45. Female sheep
46. Pale; ashen faced
47. Not poor
50. Parachutes are made of it
51. Hitler's political party
52. Expression of surprise
53. Hit with the foot or shoe
54. Therefore
59. You have one on each side
60. Same as 52 DOWN
62. Beginning and end of MEN
63. District Attorney

WORDS

AC	MUD
ADVENTUROUS	NAIL
AH	NAZI
AI	NC
AIL	NE
AL	NEVADA
AN	NEW YORK
ANT	NICE
ARGUE	NM
ARIZONA	NO
ARKANSAS	NS
ARM	NYLON
CALIFORNIA	OAK
DA	OF
DATA	OH
DO	OHIO
DOE	OK
EE	ON
ELF	ONE
EM	OVEN
EWES	OZ
FOR	RE
GS	REEL
INCHES	RICH
IS	SAID
IX	SI
KANSAS	SIN
KEEP	SON
KENTUCKY	TENNESSEE
KICK	THUS
LA	TOY
MADE	UFO
MAINE	VAIN
METRE	WA
MINT	WAN
MN	ZIP CODE
MR	

TOO MANY C's

ACROSS

1. You sit in one
2. Do not put your elbows on the _____ when you eat!
8. Opposite of IN
11. Focus on the target
12. A mixed -up crowd
13. The money in Europe
14. Short for Blood Pressure
15. Short for Mother
17. Hitler's feared police
18. Middle of BUTTER
19. Part of a bed
22. Do, Re, ____
23. Abbrev. for Northeast
25. Not FROM
26. Move shoulders up and down
28. Female sheep (sing.)
30. Where you take a bath
32. A gray color
33. Balcony; patio
36. A large primate

39. Beginning of street
40. Middle of DUCT
41. Do without
43. Against; A ledge or working surface
47. Short for ROUTE
48. Slyness; secretiveness
53. An evil deed
55. The largest city in Illinois
56. Hurt; feel poorly
57. Slang for HELLO
58. A exact genetic duplicate
59. He, she or ___
61. Against; the opposite of
64. NA backwards
65. Notes about money owed
67. Burn on the outside
68. What a person sleeps on
69. Nothing; empty
70. Calm; Make feel better
71. Lower singing voices

DOWN

1. A storage place
2. With it; in style
3. Exist
4. Water from the eye
5. First two letters of ALWAYS
6. President Truman's wife's name
7. Minus; fewer
8. Not IN
9. First letters of EUROPE
10. This night
13. AND in old Rome
15. Short for MOTHER
16. Tempt; draw to
20. Not FROM
21. Consume
22. Make a mess; stir up
24. A female sheep
27. A god in ancient Egypt
29. Emergency Room
31. One is used in baseball
34. The smallest of a litter of animals
35. A piece of jewelry for the ears
37. An outdoor room for a barbeque
38. The order of the letters after "C"
42. A couch
43. A padded seat; to make soft
44. A vase with feet
45. Repeated sound
46. Small bodies of land in water
49. The highest card; an expert
50. Ted Grunge's initials
51. Same as 21 DOWN
52. "Yes" in Spanish and Italian
54. Two in Old Rome
55. Santa _____
60. We make gasoline from it
61. Open your mouth and say "_____"!
62. Abbrev. for Not Applicable
63. ___ La, La
64. A trio of vowels
66. Very
67. Abbrev. for COUNT

68. First and last letters of BET

WORDS	
ABSTAIN	HI
ACE	HIP
AEO	II
AHH	ISLANDS
AIL	IT
AIM	LESS
AL	LT
ALTOS	IOUS
AM	MA
AN	MATTRESS
ANTI	MELEE
APE	MI
ASH	MUSS
ATTRACT	NA
BAT	NE
BED	NIL
BESS	OIL
BP	OUT
CABINET	PATIO
CHAIR	RA
CHAR	RT
CHICAGO	RUNT
CLAUS	SHRUG
CLONE	SI
COUNTER	SIN
CRAFTINESS	SO
CT	SOFA
CUSHION	SOOTH
EARRING	SS
EAT	ST
ECHO	TABLE
EI	TEAR
ER	TERRACE
ET	TG
EU	TO
EURO	TONIGHT
EWE	TRA
	TT
	UC
	UR
	URN
	TUB

AMORE IN ITALIA

ACROSS`

1. He discovered America
7. He built a boat
10. United States of America
11. LOVE in Italy
13. California
14. Short for Pamela
16. President whose first name was Ronald
19. Abbrev. for IRREGULAR
20. Kinds of plants which are smoked
21. Man's title
22. Exist
23. Pain, hurt
26. Tears
29. Vowels in trial
30. Opposite of DOWN
31. North Carolina
33. Name of two Presidents
35. Opposite of YES
36. The author's initials
37. Middle of SUIT
39. Abbrev. for GALLON
40. End letters of GIRL
41. OF, backwards
43. A scary word
45. First president's first name
47. Number on a baseball team
49. United Nations
50. Is; exist
51. Bad smell
52. Biggest name in elevators
54. Lubricant
55. Famous woman in the Bible
57. Concealed; veiled
59. Opie's aunt; short for Beatrice
61. Kind of monkey
63. Old; advanced in years
66. Abbrev. for Ralph Loren
67. One of the greatest writers in the English language

DOWN		WORDS
1. The boss of a ship	AP	ICE
2. Building material made from trees	AO	IR
3. United States	ACHE	IRL
4. One of the first explorers to China	ACID	LL
5. Droops	AGED	LUMBER
6. Opposite of DAUGHTER	A.D.	MA
7. A boy's name	ALI	MARCO POLO
8. A harsh chemical that eats surfaces	AMORE	MR
9. A book character who is studying magic	ANVIL	NC
12. Abbrev. for Master's Degree	APE	NO
15. First letters of AORTA	AOR	NED
17. Beginning of ECHO	ARE	NINE
18. First two letters of 15 DOWN	BE	NOAH
23. Block of iron used in metalworking	BEA	NOTES
24. Handle of a sword	BOO	ON
25. Consume	BUSH	OIL
27. End of girl	CA	ODOR
28. Very	CPA	OTIS
30. Same as 49 ACROSS	CAPTAIN	PA
32. Bookkeeper's advanced degree	COLUMBUS	PAM
34. New money in Europe	DR	REAGAN
38. Name of a president and a car	EA	RL
39. The boss of an army	EAT	RIPS
41. Deceive; an unwise person	EC	RUTH
42. Early man in the Bible	EURO	ROOSEVELT
43. Two presidents had this name	FO	SHAKESPEARE
44. Opposite of OFF	FOOL	SO
45. Same as 45 ACROSS	FORD	SON
46. Slang for person who runs errands	GAL	SAGS
48. Short letters	GOFER	SETH
53. Same as C.E.	GEORGE	TOBACCOS
56.Opposite of DOWN	GENERAL	UI
58. Frozen water	HID	UN
60. One of the greatest boxers in history	HILT	UP
62. Short for Papa	HARRY POTTER	US
63. First two letters of APPEAR	IA	USA
64. Abbrev. for EACH		
65. Title for a physician		

SPACES AND PLACES

ACROSS

1. Large land masses
7. Largest continent
10. United Kingdom
11. Same as 10 ACROSS
12. Father: abbrev.
13. Old name for Thailand
15. Part of a circle
18. Toward
19. Explosive stuff
21. Opposite of North
23. Burn on the outside
24. Do, Re _____
27. Exists
28. In addition
30. Same as 18 ACROSS
32. Admirer
34. Exist
35. Capital of Peru
36. First two letters of rifle
37. Opposite of WOMEN
39. Danger
40. Neighbor of Iraq
43. Abbrev. for REBEL
45. Belonging to me
46. Country south of the U.S.
48. He, she, ____
50. Same as 30 ACROSS
52. Yucky!
53. Country north of the U.S.
57. Prefix meaning INSIDE
58. Letter before EN
60. Not lose
62. A country where Spanish is spoken
65. Country group including England, France Germany, etc.
69. Dangerous snake
70. First two letters of Arnold
71. Small growth on the skin
72. Largest country in Asia
73. Same as 35 ACROSS

DOWN

1. Island nation in the Carribean
2. All right
3. Opposite of FROM
4. Opp. of South America
5. He built an ark
6. Brazil's continent
7. Largest continent
8. Glide on top of the snow
9. You have one on each side
12. Opposite of SKINNY.
14. Same as 9 DOWN
16. End of CARS
17. Metal money
20. NOT APPLICABLE: abbrev.
22. United States
25. Boot shaped country in Europe
26. Continent where the Congo is
29. Capitol of the United States
31. Short for until
33. What we breath
34. Hours from midnight to noon
38. Top of the spine
41. Exist
42. Abbrev. for NORTHEAST
44. Opposite of GIRL
45. Word for IN THE MIDDLE
47. Eleven in old Rome
49. Half of good-bye in England
51. Leaf of a tea plant
54. Country in Asia
55. Medical doctor's group
56. A person from Scotland
57. "In" in Spain and Germany
59. Opposite of OLD
61. Three in old Italy
62. Very
63. Root of I'M
64. National Rifle Association
66. University of Arizona
67. Abbrev. for RAILROAD
68. First two letters of ECHO
69. Common college degree

WORDS

AFRICA	MEXICO
AIR	MI
AM	MID
AMA	MY
AND	NA
AR	NE
ARC	NECK
ARM	NEPAL
ASIA	NEW
AT	NOAH
AUSTRALIA	NORTH AMERICA
BA	NRA
BOA	OK
BOY	PERIL
CANADA	REB
CHAR	RI
CHINA	RR
COIN	RS
CONTINENTS	SCOT
CUBA	SIAM
DC	SKI
EC	SO
EM	SOUTH AMERICA
EN	SOUTH
EUROPE	SPAIN
FAN	TA
FAT	TI
FR	TIL
I AM	TNT
ICKY	TO
III	UA
IRAN	UK
IS	US
IT	WART
ITALY	WIN
LIMA	XI
MEN	

WHERE ARE YOU FROM ?

ACROSS

1. The people from England
5. Person from Korea
9. Negative
10. German ONE
11. Short REFEREE
13. Government: abbrev.
14. Trouble; sadness
15. A kind of beer
16. First letters of SALLY
17. A country in Southeast Asia
19. Merit; deserve
21. A striped animal from Africa
23. Count: abbrev.
24. Creamy liquid to make skin soft
25. New Mexico
27. Remains of a fire
29. Bullets and such
31. People from Holland
32. A baby sound
34. Exist
35. Mexican shawl
38. Malaysian country
43. Singe
44. Attorney General: abbrev.
46. Its capitol is Lima
47. What have you been __ __
48. Short for DANIEL
50. Letter after AR
51. Beginning of the weather
53. Back of the neck
56. Opposite of HE
58. TRAIL. abbrev.
59. Emergency room
60. Middle of DIAL
61. Expression of surprise
62. Sound of a discovery
64. Same as 56 ACROSS
66. Without covering; nude
67. Same as 59 ACROSS
69. Opposite of WALK
70. A European country
71. The people in France speak it

16

DOWN

1. Where people speak English
2. A new star
3. Rules for living
4. An oral presentation
5. Oven for ceramics
6. Not two
7. Language some Arabs speak
8. Northeast
10. Organ for hearing
12. Where 71 ACROSS is spoken
16. A pair or group of items
18. Short for OLD
20. Toward
21. A place with cages for animals
22. End of BURRO
24. End of FILM
26. A Greek letter
27. Air Conditioning
28. Fired from a gun; injection
29. First two letters of AORTA
30. The big city in Russia
32. Used in England for GUY
33. A gold measurement
34. Short for Beatrice
36. Expression for "What?"
37. Signal on screen; makes a blip on a screen
38. Language spoken in Mexico and Spain
39. Middle of SUEDE
40. Mister: abbrev.
41. First two letters of AUTO
42. Language spoken in Russia
45. Language spoken in Germany
49. New Hampshire
52. Chemical used as an old anesthetic
54. Remove the skin from fruit
55. Emergency Room
57. Not soft
62. Part of a circle
63. Expression of disbelief or derision
65. Part of what Santa says
66. A college degree
68. Prefix meaning to do again

WORDS

AC	
AG	KOREAN
AHA	LAOS
ALE	LAWS
AMMO	LM
AO	LOTION
ARABIC	MOSCOW
ARC	MR.
ASH	MU
AT	NAPE
AU	NE
BA	NH
BARE	NM
BE	NO
BEA	NOVA
CHAP	OH
CHAR	OL
COO	ONE
CT	PEEL
DAN	PERU
DUTCH	RADAR
EAR	RE
EARN	REF
EH	RUN
EIN	RUSSIAN
EITHER	RO
ENGLAND	SA
ENGLISH	SET
ER	SERAPE
ES	SHE
ETHER	SHOT
FRANCE	SPANISH
FRENCH	SPEECH
GERMAN	SUMATRA
GV	TR
HARD	UE
HO	UP TO
HOLLAND	WEATH
HUH	WOE
IA	ZEBRA
KARAT	ZOO
KILN	

I'M ALL EARS

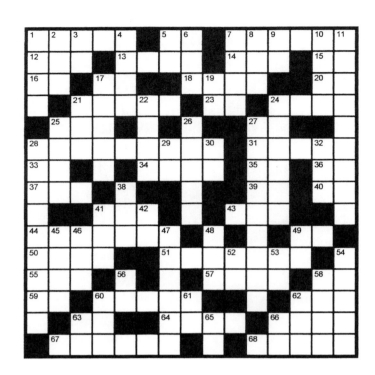

ACROSS

1. Opposite of BOYS
5. Toward
7. A circular edge
12. A short thin, round piece of metal or wood
13. Skirt for a ballerina
14. Short for RODNEY
15. A battery size
16. United Nations
17. First two letters of CURL
18. Laced up; made into a knot
20. Abbrev. for railroad
21. Jewish spiritual leader; Jewish teacher
23. Singing syllable
24. Pleasant
25. Opposite of NEAR
27. Abbrev. for COLORADO
28. Not nothing
31. Overhead
33. A river in Europe
34. Put words to a tune
35. Opposite of FROM
36. Four in old Rome
37. Consumed
39. Abbrev. for hard drive
40. Two in Roman Numerals
41. What a cow says
43. Male child
44. Small salty body of water connected to a sea
49. A kind of candy
50. Scooted
51. Greed for money
55. Not HERS
57. Opposite of FRONT
58. Half of what Santa says
59. Part of the personality
60. Sixteen ounces make one
62. Glass container
63. Letter before "S"
64. You eat them if they're corn
66. Plural for 62 ACROSS
67. Same as 7 ACROSS
68. A big crowd

18

DOWN	WORDS	
1. Slang for FOOD	AA	JARS
2. Charged atom	ABOVE	JO
3. Short for ROAD	AR	LA
4. A blunt end of something	AREA	LAB
5. Middle of the bottle	AROUND	ME
6. Not in	ATE	MM
7. Length times width	AVARICE	MOO
8. Same as 14 ACROSS	BACK	MUD
9. To take too much of something	BAHS	NARC
10. Short for a kind of policeman	BOA	NICE
11. A person who takes unsafe chances	BOY	NOBODY
17. Troubled; felt for	CARED	OD
19. Beginning of ILLNESS	CATHOLICS	OR
21. Male sheep	CK	OUT
22. They come before HUMBUGS	CO	PO
24. Not somebody	CU	POUND
25. Twelve inches; what we walk on	DA	PRO
26. Not OUTER	DAREDEVIL	RA
27. Members of Pope's church	EARS	RABBI
28. What space aliens ride in	ESTUARY	RAM
29. Two in old Rome	FAR	RD
30. Short for GREAT-GRANDMOTHER	FOOT	RM
32. Seven times one in Rome	GG	ROD
38. A dangerous snake	GIRLS	RR
41. Wet dirt	GRUB	SING
42. Partner of EITHER	HARD	SLID
45. Scooted	HD	SO
46. Same as 50 ACROSS	HIS	SOMETHING
47. Opened position; wide open	HO	SPACESHIP
48. Where experiments are done	HORDE	STUB
49. Not you	HORSE	TIED
52. An Egyptian god	ID	TIS
53. Back of BACK	II	TO
54. An animal that is usually ridden	IL	TT
56. Very	INNER	TUTU
58. Not easy	ION	UN
60. Expert at a golf course	IV	VII
61. Attorney for the people	JAR	YAWNED
62. Same as 62 ACROSS		
63. Letter before "S"		
65. Short for ROOM		
66. Short for Josephine		

19

CHESS OR GOLF ?

ACROSS

1. A game played with balls and clubs
5. Game played on a court
12. Shapes of eggs
14. United Nations
15. You row with one
16. A young man
17. Cultivate; plant
20. King of the jungle
21. Game played with goal posts at each end of a field
24. Colorado
26. Nuke; heat in a microwave
27. THE in Spanish and Italian
28. Place to work out; building for exercise
29. Full of energy
30. Short for Beatrice
32. A common college degree
33. Scored in wrestling
35. Ending word in a prayer

36. Tool used for smoothing
39. Ovum
40. Frozen water
41. Very fast
44. Abbrev. for "that is"
45. All right
46. Air Conditioning
48. Wide shoe size
49. Eliminate; erase
51. Slash; cut
55. Same as B.C.E.
56. A famous tennis player
57. Spirit
58. Throat sound used to get attention
59. Letter after R
60. Letter before D
61. Catholic religious service
62. Some people get this way in airplanes
66. Two vowels
67. A football position
68. Every year; on a yearly basis

DOWN

1. Where you play golf
2. Eggs in science
3. Opposite of gentleman
4. Beginning of FLOOD
6. Car; short for automobile
7. A pout; mildly upset
8. Opposite of FROM
9. Round object used in games; a formal dance
10. Short for Aristotle
11. Football position
13. African jungle trip
18. Sixteen ozs make one
19. Tra, ___, ___
22. Unlocked; ajar
23. THE in Spanish and Italian
25. Opposite of OFF
26. A closing and opening device
28. A recreational activity
30. Set out; start
31. Rim; side; border
32. A game played with a board and disks
34. Northeast
37. A kind of monkey; a primate
38. Southeast
40. The vowels in BOIL
42. Bother; interrupt
43. Short for YARD
46. What's left after a fire
47. A game played with a board and "men"
50. Hurt
52. "B" __ in BOY
53. True; faithful
54. Funny person; one who cracks jokes
55. Not the FRONT
57. Play around (With OFF)
63. First two letter of ILLNESS
64. AS, backwards
65. End of BACK
66. Common prefix as in ENCLOSE

WORDS

AC	GOLF COURSE
ACHE	GOOF
AHEM	GYM
AIR SICK	ICE
AMEN	IE
ANNUAL	IL
APE	IO
ARI	LA LA
AS	LA
ASHE	LAD
ASHES	LADY
AUTO	LB
BA	LINEMAN
BACK	LION
BACKGAMMON	LOYAL
BALL	MASS
BASKETBALL	NE
BC	OAR
BEA	OK
BEGIN	ON FIRE
CE	ON
CHESS	OPEN
CK	OVA
CO	OVALS
COMIC	PINNED
DISTURB	RASP
EDGE	RID
EE	SA
EGG	SAFARI
EN	SE
EO	SNIT
ES	SPEEDY
FL	TILL
FOOTBALL	TO
FULLBACK	UN
GAME	YD
GASH	ZAP
GHOST	ZIPPER
GOLF	

ATOM OR ION

ACROSS

1. An Irish elf
5. One of santa's helpers
7. A spirit form
11. Nickname for Aristotle
12. The edge of an opening
14. Opposite of NONE
16. Also
17. Abbrev. for Railroad
18. Some vowels
19. Exist
20. Machine to increase volume
21. A kind of tea. Part of a martial art
23. Scottish NO
24. Slang for HELLO or OK
26. Open wide and say _____
27. Opposite of SHE
28. Ancient Egyptian god
29. Hurrah!
31. Opposite of STOOD
33. First two letters of the alphabet
35. Hitler's secret police
37. Abbrev. for North Dakota
39. Not nice; rude
41. Two vowels

42. Act
43. Encountered; came together
44. Also
45. Old metal gets _____ on it
48. Opposite of "no SIR"
51. A charged atom
53. Circular in shape
55. A small insect that stings
56. Same as 55 ACROSS
57. Two vowels
58. A religious trip to Mecca
60. Near
62. A pinching underwater creature
63. Female sheep
64. Nickname for ABRAHAM
66. Short for MOTHER
67. First two letters of ASTRONOMY
68. Short for LITTLE
70. University of Arizona
71. Fourteen in old Rome
72. Hat worn for protection
75. Northeast
76. Myself; opposite of YOU
77. Puzzled; can't figure something out

DOWN

1. Celebration
2. Abbrev. for IRRIGATION
3. Eleven in old Italy
4. One of the largest animals on earth
5. Certain period of time
6. Do, Re, Mi, ___
7. A room or building for exercise
8. Not this; short for ANOTHER
9. Very
10. How to score in football
13. Two in the Roman Empire
15. First two letters of NAVY
18. Accumulate a lot
22. Opposite of COLD
25. Not off
30. Opposite of OR
32. Short for an animated movie
34. Near; close
36. Help letters
38. One who is a citizen of America
40. Same as 16 ACROSS
45. A small rodent; a bad person
46. Very small
47. Can't do; not capable
49. Title for a king: "Your
   _____"
50. Adjective indicating ONE
52. First two letters of OTHER
54. Opposite of MINE
56. Lincoln was called "Honest ___"
58. Steering wheel of a ship
59. Expression of dismay
61. Kept for the future; prevented
   from dying
64. My mother's sister is my _____
65. Common college degree
66. Opposite of OURS
69. Sick
72. A male pronoun
73. Letter after "L"
74. Word of uncertainty

WORDS

AB	II
ABE	LIL
AEIO	LIP
AH	LO
AM	MA
AMASS	MAJESTY
AMERICAN	ME
AMP	MET
AN	MINE
AND	MYSTIFIED
ANT	NA
ANY	NAE
ARI	ND
AS	NE
AUNT	NO MA'AM
AW	ON
BA	OT
BY	OTHER
CHI	OURS
CRAB	PARTY
DO	PIXIE
ELEPHANT	RA
ELF	RAH
EM	RAT
EPOCH	ROUND
EWE	RR
FA	RUST
GHOST	SAT
GYMNASIUM	SAVED
HAJ	SNOTTY
HE	SO
HEAT	SOS
HELM	SS
HELMET	TINY
IF	TOO
II	TOON
IO	TOUCHDOWN
ION	UA
IRR	UNABLE
IU	XI
ILL	XIV
	YO

TASTY

STUFF

ACROSS

1. Italian pie
5. Flapjacks
12. Opposite of OFF
13. Letter after R
14. Primate
15. Sags before dying
17. Liquid for writing
19. Short for Father
21. Fifth letter of the alphabet
22. Pronoun for a thing
23. Sensed
24. Two in ancient Rome
25. Toward
26. Music, painting, sculpture, etc.
28. Short for trail
29. Same as B.C.E.
30. Same as C.E.
31. Consumed
32. Exist
33. Furry animal in the woods
36. Opposite of ques.
38. Old-fashioned; had dates with
40. Large shrimp

42. Used to find the area of a circle
43. Prim and proper; set in one's ways
44. Expression of delight
45. Same as BC
47. Round pastry with a filling
49. Abbrev. For Grade Point
     Average
51. Meat from a pig
53. Shut with force
55. Strangle
56. Game played on horseback;
     a kind of shirt
57. Opposite of she
58. Large, strong tree
59. Pastry with icing
61. Same as 31 ACROSS
63. Tra-La-_ _
64. Sour
66. Method of remembering
69. Open wide and say_ _
70. Consume
71. Opposite of OUT
72. Method of cooking food

DOWN

1. Hawaiian dish
2. Motel or hotel
3. Last letter of the alphabet
4. Kind of snake
5. What you write on
6. Abbrev. For APPLICATION
7. Tidy
8. Rueful expression
9. Green, fuzzy fruit
10. Room extension; elevated railway
11. In place of; in _ _ _ _ of
16. A pair; a group that goes together
18. A toy that flies in the air
20. Many times
24. A cool drink made from leaves
26. A battery size
27. Short for ROUTE
29. Ammunition for an air gun
30. A vegetable with leaves and a good heart
32. A stringed musical instrument
34. Another battery size
35. Same as CE
37. Kind of pasta
39. Short for EDWARD
40. A frozen treat
41. Stir up
43. South Carolina
45. Cook in an oven
46. Without bumps or rough areas
48. Abbrev. for EACH
50. A river in Italy
52. Short for ALFRED
54. Encounter; come together
55. Burn on the outside
56. Short for FATHER
60. A battery size
62. Opposite of against
65. Exist
67. Opposite of FROM
68. Same as 48 DOWN

WORDS

AA	INK
AAA	INN
A.D.	IT
AH	KITE
AL	KIWI
AM	LA
ANS	MEET
APE	NEAT
APPL	OAK
ART	OFTEN
ARTICHOKE	ON
ASP	OO
AT	PA
ATE	PANCAKES
AW	PAPER
BAKE	PI
BANJO	PIE
BB	PIZZA
B.C.	PO
B.C.E.	POI
BE	POLO
BEAR	POPPA
CAKE	POPSICLE
CHAR	PRAWN
CHOKE	ROAST
DATED	ROIL
DROOPS	ROTE
EA	RT
EAT	SC
ED	SET
EE	SLAM
EL	SMOOTH
ES	SPAGHETTI
FELT	STAID
FOR	STEAD
GPA	TART
HAM	TO
HE	TR
ICED TEA	WILTS
II	ZE
IN	

THE TECH AGE

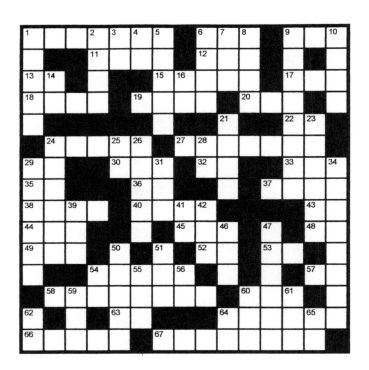

ACROSS

1. Machine that types out computer entries
6. Colored liquid or powder used in printers and pens
9. Owns
11. Both a vegetable and a stew
12. Once named
13. Personal Computer
15. Opposite of Mommy
17. Part of the name of a famous volcano
18. Put designs on glass with acid
19. A large town
20. Help letters
22. Opposite of FROM
24. Change gears
27. Machine that loads images onto a computer
29. THE in Spanish
30. Able; in shape
32. A metric measurement often used in science and medicine
33. Nurses
35. Exist
36. Do, Re, Mi, __ __
37. As soon as possible: abbrev.
38. Prod; thrust forward
40. Opposite of HAND
43. You in Spanish
44. Beverage brewed with leaves
45. Short for FACSIMILE
48. Abbrev. for EACH
49. Opposite of NEW
52. Eleven in old Italy
53. Same as 35 ACROSS
54. Strong rope; cord to carry signals
57. Myself
58. A branch of Mathematics dealing with shapes
60. Set cost for service
63. Spanish and Italian for IN
64. First name of a ride at the fair
66. Electrical "ropes" used to connect machines
67. Instructions written for a computer

DOWN

1. What you write on
2. He built a boat for two-by-two creatures
3. First and last letters of TACK
4. Emergency Room
5. Machine which receives on radio sound signals
6. Big car race in the U.S.
7. A boy's name
8. What you type on or open a door with
9. Leather holders for guns
10. Transfer an image into pixels
14. Connecticut
16. Present on the spot
21. Individually
22. Very fancy; with lots of decoration
24. One of the prophets in the Bible
25. Fast Forward
26. Small arguments
28. Metric measurement usually used for medicine
29. Small, portable computer
31. A Far East philosophy of correct behavior
34. What gives off the sound on a computer or player
39. Blue; unhappy
41. From
42. Money collected by the government to pay its
     expenses
46. Twelve in Old Rome
47. It takes pictures
50. Leisure pastimes in a box
51. Elevation: abbrev.
54. Colorado
55. Short for BENJAMIN
56. Same as 4 DOWN
59. Hearing organ
60. Opposite of MANY
61. Short for ERROR
62. Same as B.C.E.
64. Foot: abbrev.
65. "That is" or "such as"

WORDS

ALT	KEYS
AM	LA
ASAP	LAPTOP
AT	LE
BC	LOA
BEN	ME
CABLE	NED
CAMERA	NEE
CC	NOAH
CITY	OF
CO	OKRA
CORDS	OLD
CT	ORNATE
DADDY	PAPER
EA	PC
EACH	PRINTER
EAR	PUSH
EN	RADIO
ER	RNS
ERR	SAD
ETCH	SAMUEL
FA	SCAN
FAX	SCANNER
FEE	SHIFT
FERRIS	SOFTWARE
FEW	SOS
FF	SPEAKERS
FIT	TAO
FOOT	TAX
FT	TE
GAMES	TEA
GEOMETRY	TIFFS
HAS	TK
HOLSTERS	TO
IE	XI
INDY	XII

INK

27

WHO'S WHO

ACROSS

1. My daughter's husband
8. Opposite of FATHER
11. Receive money or property after a death
12. Short for SMALL
14. Prefix meaning inside
15. Part of a laugh
17. A small ocean
19. Mexican dish rolled in a corn husk
23. A female child
25. Not here
26. Initials for Donald Moore
27. Beams (like an X-ray)
28. Expression like GEE
31. Esteem; commend
34. Number before TWO
35. Opposite of MOTHER
39. My son's son
44. Not this, but the _____

45. Myself
46. Part of a minute; small amount of time
47. Dam; channel; enclosure
48. Opposite of out
49. Ancient Egyptian pagan god
51. Spanish for YOU
52. Eleven to Julius Caesar
55. Middle of SUEDE
57. Joke with words
58. Existed
60. Not Applicable
61. Those with the least amount of money
63. Opposite of FRONT
64. Repeated sound
66. A high peak or mountain
67. One who inherits
68. Opposite of AUNT
69. Short for FATHER

DOWN

1. Opposite of BROTHER
2. First two letters of NIGHT
3. My husband's parents and family
4. New Hampshire
5. THE in French
6. Exist
7. Air that is moving
9. Hurry
10. Sound a lion makes
13. Short for MOTHER
15. Make vocal music without words
16. Attorney General
18. A wide shoe width
20. Have permission
21. THE in Spanish and Italian
22. Organ for seeing
24. One who adds
29. Move; operate
30. Rage; ire
31. Esteem, commend
32. The smallest of a litter of animals
33. Where a battle was fought in the Bible
35. Wealth
36. Consumed
37. Not those
38. Male pronoun
40. Exist
41. Same as 26 ACROSS
42. Put down; lay down
43. Fifty-two minus fifty-three
50. Chopping tools
53. Suffix that means one who believes in
      something
54. Posed a question
57. Name for a boy or a girl
58. Department of a hospital
59. Air Conditioning
61. Food used by the old Hawaiians
62. Sound of pain
63. Little ___ Peep
65. Same as 38 DOWN
66. Same as 51 ACROSS

WORDS

AC	JEST
ADDER	LA
AG	LE
AM	MA
ANGER	MAY
ARE	ME
ASKED	MOMENT
ATE	MOTHER
AWAY	NA
AXES	NH
BACK	NI
BO	ONE
DAUGHTER	OTHER
GRANDSON	OW
DAD	POI
DM	POOREST
EACH	RA
ECHO	RAYS
EE	REE
EGAD	REMAIN
EN	ROAR
EYE	RUNT
FATHER	SEA
FORTUNE	SET
GO	SISTER
HA	SM
HASTEN	SON-IN-LAW
HE	TAMALE
HEIR	TE
HONOR	THEM
HUM	TOR
IN	UE
INHERIT	UNCLE
IN-LAWS	WARD
IST	WAS
JEAN	WIND
JERICHO	XI

WHAT'S THE WORD ?

ACROSS

1. Names of persons, places or things
5. Action word
8. It's a baby girl's color
12. Prefix that means inside
13. The countries west of Asia
15. Prefix meaning ALMOST; a large truck
16. Letter after "U"
17. A large rodent that sometimes carries diseases
18. Information for use
20. Northeast
21. Short for EACH
23. Opposite of SOFT
26. A rest period; A school play period
30. Mixture of dirt and water
31. Book with words and their meanings
35. Organ for hearing
36. Sharpen
38. Carry around
42. Sound of delight
43. Beginning of ENCLOSE
44. A ship that moves under the water
47. Opposite of AND
48. What a person or thing is called
50. Decipher; interpret
52. Put words on paper
54. You fix your hair with it
56. A kind of fruit with a hard shell
57. Opposite of GOOD
58. The last one
59. Same as 47 ACROSS
61. A small island
62. _____, white and blue
64. A small globe
66. The color of most plants
67. A word that describes something

DOWN

1. Opposite of ALWAYS
2. How many noses do you have?
3. Northeast
4. The most secure
5. Cast a ballot
6. The end of JEEP
7. Same as 62 ACROSS
8. A song or prayer in the Bible
9. That is: abbrev.
10. New Mexico
11. Gentle; nice
14. Ancient Egyptian pagan god
19. Muscle in you stomach
20. Between you head and you torso
22. Many teens have this condition
24. Middle of LOUD
25. End of THUD
27. Short for EDUCATION
28. 101 in old Rome
29. Opposite of STAND
32. A battery size
33. Short for RAILROAD
34. Horrible; ful of terror
36. You dig weeds with it
37. Sound of delight
38. The act of absorbing information
39. United Nations
40. Make music without words
41. I AM
42. Single
44. Opposite of HAPPY
45. Be careful; watch out!
46. Fare; price
48. Locally born and grown
49. A miniature Japanese tree
51. European Union
53. Short for ROAD
54. 102 for Brutus
55. Prefix for bad or evil
57. Came into existence
60. Raw metal
63. District Attorney
64. Short for orange juice

66. Same as B.C.E.

WORDS

AA	MUD	
AB	NAME	
ACNE	NATIVE	
ADJECTIVE	NE	
BAD	NECK	
BC	NEVER	
BEWARE	NM	
BONSAI	NOUNS	
BORN	NUT	
CI	OJ	
CII	ONE	
COMB	OO	
DA	OOO	
DATA	OR	
DICTIONARY	ORE	
EA	ORB	
EAR	OU	
ED	PINK	
EN	PSALM	
EP	RA	
EU	RAT	
EUROPE	RATE	
FINAL	RD	
GREEN	READ	
HOE	RECESS	
HONE	RED	
HUM	RR	
IE	SAD	
I'M	SEMI	
ISLE	SIT	
KIND	SUBMARINE	
LEARNING	SUREST	
LOUD	TERRIBLE	
LUG	UD	
MAL	UN	
	VEE	
	VERB	
	VOTE	
	WRITE	

AMID

THE

WORDS

ACROSS

1. A group of players in a sport
4. Number on a baseball team
7. Where you play tennis
10. Short for RUSSIA
12. Above
14. Prefix for "over again"
15. Make a difference
17. Emergency Room
18. Uncertain word
20. First two letters of BACK
21. Television
22. Short for ERROR
23. Roman Numeral two
24. The leader of the Confederate army
25. Southeast
26. Top of; over
28. You do it on snow
30. Not HE or SHE
31. A nurse's degree
32. Metal found in the earth
33. Opposite of HERS
35. Cruel; not nice
36. THE in Spanish
38. It's made of dirt

42. Smell; usually a bad one
45. Northeast
46. In the middle of
48. That is: abbrev.
49. Court; flirt with
51. Opposite of BEGINNING
53. You sleep in one when camping
54. Half of GOOD-BY in England
55. Question
56. Abbrev. For Attorney General
58. Organ for hearing
60. Same as C.E.
62. Be indebted to
64. A woman's name from the Bible
67. Slang for HELLO or OK
68. Do, Re, ___
69. The red planet
70. Public Address system
71. Short for EDUCATION
73. Hand position for fighting
75. Large: abbrev.
77. A pastry with a hole in the middle
78. Not a mountain or a plain; a small rise
      in the ground
79. Exaggeration to get attention

DOWN

1. Rolling over and over
2. Music, painting, poetry, etc.
3. Mumble under one's breath
5. Opposite of YES
6. Always
7. First two letters of CRANE
8. Railroad
9. Game played on a court with rackets
11. The number after six
13. Mistake
16. A battery size
18. Roman numeral two
19. A creature that lives in the water
22. Middle of KEEP
25. Use the eyes
27. Must have
29. A kind of parrot
32. Over
34. Middle of TOOK
35. A doctor's degree
37. Lingers; dawdles
39. Kangaroos in Australia
40. United Nations
41. Same as 27 DOWN
42. A poem that praises
43. A prefix that means "over again"
44. A beverage made with boiled leaves
46. Beginning of ADMIRE
47. Pronoun for an object
49. Cautioned
50. All right
52. Bible name of a woman
54. Catch
57. Myself
59. Middle of MAIL
61. Act; accomplish
63. Hope; desire
64. A shopping area
65. Short for IRRIGATION
66. Partner for reproduction
72. Same as 61 DOWN
73. FOOT: abbrev.
74. Leaf of a tea plant
76. Near

WORDS

AA	MATTER
AI	MD
AMID	ME
ART	MEAN
ASK	MI
BA	MIRIAM
BY	NAOMI
COURT	NE
CR	NEED
DA	NINE
DO	NO
DONUT	ODE
EAR	ODOR
ED	OKAY
EE	ON
EL	OO
END	ORE
ER	OVER
ERR	OWE
ERROR	PA
EVER	RE
FISH	RN
FIST	ROOS
FT	RR
GROUND	RUS
HILL	SE
HIS	SEE
HYPE	SEVEN
IE	SKI
IF	TA
II	TEA
IRG	TEAM
IT	TENNIS
KIA	TENT
LEE	TI
LG	TRAP
LOITERS	TUMBLING
MALL	TV
MARS	UN
MATE	WARNED
	WOO
	YO

WHAT IS IT?

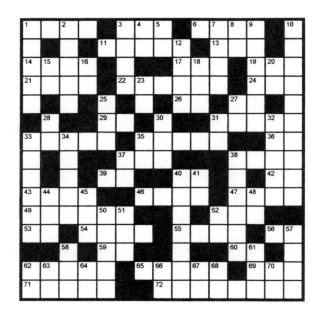

ACROSS

1. Opposite of LOW
3. The opposite of 1 ACROSS
6. Not UP
11. Main artery in the heart
13. Letter before "W"
14. Vista; scene
17. Famous Confederate general
19. What we breathe
21. Opposite of west
22. One who operates a vehicle
24. Bind; fasten; knot
26. First two vowels
27. Myself
29. Not YES
31. Belief; dogma
33. Have to; tied up
35. Not an adult; a teenager
36. Spanish for BULL
37. Suffix for THE MOST
39. Ancient pagan god in Egypt

40. A common college degree
42. First letters of Anthony
43. Notion; thought
46. Partly open
47. Voices; utters; speaks
49. With tiny splotches all over
52. Suffix meaning a belief
53. Prefix that means inside
54. Popular island in the Hawaiian
      Islands
55. A famous tennis player
56. Sound of surprise
59. First two letters of ROBERT
60. District Attorney
61. A fuss
62. Without life or movement
66. A muscle in the upper arm
69. Abbrev. for December
71. Not South
72. Working together to accomplish a
      common purpose

DOWN

1. Float just above
2. A person who is visiting
3. Not soft
4. Partner of EITHER
5. Abbrev. for WEIGHT
7. Above
8. Us
9. Straighten up
10. Instructions on how to get someplace
12. Thomas Edison's middle name
15. Weight: abbrev.
18. A very wide shoe size
20. Two to Caesar
23. Same as 39 ACROSS
25. AND in German
27. Not you
28. Not from
30. The thing over a small "I"
31. Suffix for numbers
32. A picture of your insides
33. Next to
34. Knocked over; emotional
35. Abbrev. for year
37. Each
38. Gently thrown
40. Even; scale; equality
41. Letter before "S"
45. Machine that gives cash from your account
48. Toward
50. Our planet
51. A set of two
52. HI backwards
57. A writer; chop
58. Ocean in French
61. A fuss;
62. Not out
63. Opposite of YES
64. Abbrev. for ROUTE
66. He, she or ___
67. Each
68. The hours between noon and midnight
70. Emergency Room

WORDS

ADO	IN
E	INERT
AIR	IST
AJAR	IT
ALVA	LA
AN	LEE
AORTA	LH
AR	LOUD
ASHES	LOW
AT	MAUI
ATM	ME
BA	MER
BALANCE	NEATEN
BESIDE	NO
BICEPS	NORTH
BOUND	OH
DA	OR
DEC	OVER
DIRECTIONS	PM
DON	RA
DOT	RO
DOTTED	RT
DOWN	SAYS
DRIVER	TEAMWORK
DUO	TENET
EA	TH
EARTH	TIE
EAST	TO
EEE	TORO
EN	TOSSED
ER	UND
EST	UPSET
EXRAY	VEE
GUEST	VIEW
HACK	WE
HIGH	WT
HOVER	XI
IA	YOUTH
IDEA	YS
II	

SCHOOL

DAYS

ACROSS
1. A certain group of students
5. Used to write with on a chalkboard
8. Stomach muscle
10. THE in Spanish and Italian
11. Help; assist
13. Exist
14. Letter before "EN"
16. Not fronts or backs
18. A kind of candy
21. A learner
23. One who gives instruction
26. Short for Samuel
27. Swap; business
29. They are needed with a canoe
30. Short for ROUTE
31. A wiggly letter
33. Emergency Room
34. It has an engine and a caboose
35. People have one on each side
36. A slithery fish
37. A baby's bed
39. Not IN
41. Short for TON

42. Expression of surprise
43. A shoe width
44. Same as 18 ACROSS
45. A small child
47. A camping house
50. A kind of firearm
52. An evergreen tree
53. Short for height
55. A light brown color used in art and
    photography
57. A country next to Iraq
59. Mistake
61. THE in Spanish
62. Get possession again
64. United Nations
65. A famous movie actor
67. The night before
68. "M" in Greece
69. Very
70. Toward
71. Organ for seeing
72. Absorb information; begin to
    understand

DOWN

1. A room for learning
2. THE in Spanish and Italian
3. Spoken; uttered
4. Not the top or the bottom
6. Part of a laugh
7. Exist
9. Exist
12. Depression; imprint
15. The red planet
16. Total; result of addition
17. Avenue; thoroughfare
18. Encounter
19. Short for MOTHER
20. An object for sitting
22. Make lace
23. Touchdown: abbrev.
24. One who teaches; usually in sports
25. A character on Sesame Street
28. Are not
31. Same as 33 ACROSS
32. Not rough
35. Toward
38. A grizzly is one
40. Referee
42. Not this one, but the _____
45. A famous poet's first two initials
46. Small child
48. Prefix meaning inside or surrounded by
49. Hushed; silence
51. Angry
52. Not last
54. Letter before "es"
55. Opposite of DAUGHTER
56. 'Oh, dear!"
58. Apse; hub
60. Govern; a measuring tool; a law
63. What is played on the piano; used to lock up
65. The source of heat on the earth
66. Decay; go bad
68. Mister

WORDS

AB	MEET
AID	MM
ALAS	MR
AM	MU
AR	NAVE
AREN'T	OARS
ARM	OH
AT	OTHER
BE	OUT
BEAR	PISTOL
CHALK	QUIET
CHAIR	RETAKE
CLASS	ROT
CLASSROOM	RT
COACH	RULE
CRIB	SAID
DENT	SAM
EE	SEPIA
EEL	SIDE
EL	SIDES
EM	SMOOTH
EN	SO
ER	SON
ERNIE	STAR
ERROR	STREET
ES	STUDENT
EVE	SUM
EYE	SUN
FIR	TAT
FIRST	TD
HA	TEACHER
HT	TENT
IRAN	TN
IRATE	TO
KEY	TOT
LA	TRADE
LEARN	TRAIN
MA	TS
MARS	UMPIRE
	UN

YOU

LAZY

OAF

ACROSS

1. Short for UNTIL
4. The first man in the Bible
6. Not expensive
10. Sometimes called "Black Gold"
11. Organ for hearing
12. Part of the personality
14. Having life
16. Short for ORGANIZATION
17. Same as 11 ACROSS
18. An injection; firing from a gun
20. Fool; dunce
23. Do, Re, Mi,_____
24. Less expensive
25. Make lace
27. Old French money
30. The highest cards in a deck; pros
33. Exist

35. Assist; aid
36. He built a boat in the Bible
37. One of the Three Stooges
39. Period of time; a certain age
40. Discomfort; Ache
44. Encounter
46. Accomplish; act
47. One who takes are of cattle
50. Six to Caesar
51. Friend
53. Flirt with; romance
54. Three in old Rome
56. Negative
58. Female sheep
60. Fish egg
61. A small speck
62. Prefix meaning NOT

DOWN

1. Also
2. Two in Ancient Italy
3. The Author's initials
4. Old saying with a lesson in it
5. Change position; go forward
6. Same as A.D.
7. Head covering
8. Emergency Room
9. Number used to find measurements of a circle
13. Pay excessive attention to
15. Comfortable; without difficulty
16. From
19. A four legged animal that can be ridden
20. Frequently
21. A small battery size
22. Secretly watch or listen
26. Air Conditioning
28. Middle of the hole
29. Opposite of DOWN
30. Sound of contentment
31. Give off
32. Very
34. Opposite of WOMEN
35. Opposite of SAD
38. Arm joint
41. Same as 12 ACROSS
42. Idea; thought
43. Lid; overhead protection
44. Third sound on a scale
45. A deer-like animal from Africa
48. Troubles; problems
49. Arrows are shot with it
52. Bathroom in England
54. Charged atom
55. Myself
57. Middle of butter
59. A wide width

WORDS

AAA	LL
AC	LOO
ACES	ME
ADAGE	MEET
ADAM	MEN
AH	MI
ALIVE	MOE
AM	MOVE
BOW	NOAH
CE	NON
CHEAP	NOT
CHEAPER	NOTION
COVER	OF
COWBOY	OFTEN
DD	OIL
DO	OL
DOT	OAF
DOTE	ORG
EAR	PAIN
EASE	PAL
EE	PALE
ELAND	PI
ELBOW	ROE
EMIT	SHOT
ER	SO
ERA	SOU
EWE	SPY
FA	TAT
HAPPY	TIL
HAT	TOO
HELP	TT
HORSE	UP
ID	VI
II	WOES
III	WOO
ION	

WHAT IS YOUR AGENDA ?

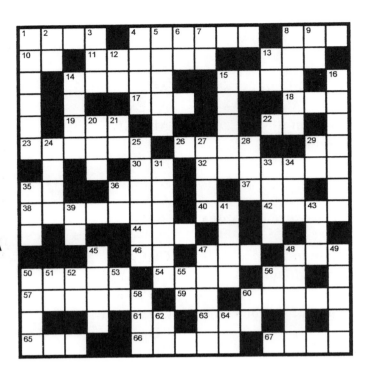

ACROSS

1. Give aid to
4. Root word for ASSISTANCE
8. Give help to
10. A thing
11. Tell
13. The night before
14. Expensive rock
15. A girl's name
17. Opposite of HAPPY
18. Letters used for owing money
19. A Scottish man's name (means John)
22. Short for ALBERT
23. Ease; comfort
26. Performance by two persons
29. Opposite of DOWN
30. Tra, La, __
32. Professional help with no charge; for the good of the community
35. A battery size
36. Droop
37. A large weight
38. Get better
40. Abbreviation for Northeast
42. Take time out to relax
44. Less than two
46. Abbreviation for ROAD
47. In the past
48. A television network
50. Crawl slowly
54. Opposite of LEGS
56. The letter before "S"
57. Except
59. Do, Re, __
60. You sit in it
61. Prefix meaning NOT
63. What you do with a chair
65. A kind of shade tree
66. Raise; make higher
67. Just; equal (an old-fashioned word)

DOWN

1. Make harder; put something in the way
2. Old Roman word for AND
3. Prefix meaning before
4. Kinds of beer
5. A dish made with greens and dressing
6. Abbreviation for STREET
7. Abbrev. for words meaning "For Example"
8. Use; help yourself
9. Such as; that is
12. Last letters of FEW
13. Prefix for INSIDE
14. A small prison
15. Not before
16. Brace; uphold; help
20. Help
21. Northeast
24. Test
25. A kind of taste
27. On top of
28. A small child
29. United Nations; prefix meaning UNDO
31. List of items for a meeting
33. Dull; uninteresting person
34. Less than two
35. Assist
36. Very
39. Short for Father
41. Chickens lay them
43. An underwater boat; a sandwich
45. Leak slowly
47. Wrong; something in error
48. Wooden box
49. Help; wait on
50. Heal; make go away
51. A nurse's degree
52. Addition to a building;
53. Initials for POST-SCRIPT
55. Short for ROOM
56. Open wide and say "____"
58. Short for SUBMARINE
60. Abbreviation for "COUNT"
62. Negative;
64. A thing

WORDS

AA	IOU
AFTER	IT
AGENDA	JAIL
AGO	JEWEL
AH	LA
AID	METE
AL	MI
ALES	NE
AMISS	NO
ANNA	ONE
AR	PA
ARMS	PRE
ASSIST	PRO BONO
AVAIL	PS
BOOST	RD
BORE	RELATE
CBS	RELIEF
CHAIR	REST
CRATE	RM
CREEP	RN
CT	SAD
CURE	SAG
DUET	SALAD
EGGS	SEEP
EL	SERVE
ELM	SIT
EN	SO
ET	ST
EVE	SUB
EW	SUPPORT
EXAM	TON
FLAVOR	TOT
HELP	UN
HINDER	UNLESS
IAN	UP
IE	UPON
IMPROVE	

HE WHO TEACHES LEARNS TWICE

ACROSS

1. A person who gives instruction
6. Childhood stage of a frog
13. Opposite of OR
14. Withheld; refrained from
15. Opposite of CREDIT
17. Letter after "EL"
19. Eleven in old Rome
20. Sheets and pillow cases and blankets
24. Short letter
27. Opposite of CLOSE
29. First two letters of ANTHEM
30. A pad of paper
33. Short for FATHER
35. Ancient Egyptian god
36. Ancient Greek god
38. Short for ROAD
39. Emergency Room
41. Leaf of a tea plant
42. Two vowels
43. Opposite of YOUR
44. One who types, files and answers the phone

48. A vehicle that carries people
50. A short sleep
52. Abbrev. for NOT APPLICABLE
53. Opposite of water; ground
54. Burn up
57. District of Columbia; our nation's capitol
58. From
59. Not far
61. Middle of HUFF
63. Picture taken of the inside of the body
65. All lined up in ___
67. First two letters of ILL
68. A tool for chopping wood
69. Short for OLD
70. The second and third letters of BOTTLE
71. Southeast
72. Make music with the voice
73. Moves away; sails; steers
74. The first man

42

DOWN

1. Special ability
2. First letters of ENVELOPE
3. Combine (in Math)
4. Center of action
5. Relationship between amounts
6. Poet Elliot's initials
7. Be present at
8. District Attorney
9. Used to find diameter of a circle
10. Opposite of OFF
11. Put weight on or against; not fat
12. Editor
16. Nine in the Roman Empire
18. Low sound of pain or sadness
20. Exist
21. Slang for FATHER
22. Opposite of OUT
23. Mechanism with cogs that turn
25. Short for tuberculosis
26. Make happy or glad
28. Operator of an airplane
31. Of large importance or size
32. Opposite of FROM
34. A large group of soldiers
35. A lot of summer TV
37. Head of the Confederate army
40. Move to music
44. Lance; sharp pointed weapon
45. A method of memorization
46. Opposite of OR
47. Persons who hate because of race
48. Confused; mixed up
49. South Dakota
51. Letter before "S"
53. First name of the author of <u>Little Women</u>
55. An amount; all; every
56. Not late
60. First two letters of ROMANCE
62. A small unit of matter
63. Twenty-one in old Rome
64. Month before Sept.
66. Fantastic! Unbelievable!
68. First two letters of ASTOR

WORDS

ABSTAINED	LOUISA
ADAM	MOAN
ADD	MY
AN	NA
AND	NAP
ANY	NEAR
APOLLO	NOTE
AR	OF
ARMY	OL
AS	ON
ATOM	OPEN
ATTEND	OT
AUG	PI
AX	PILOT
BAFFLED	RA
BE	RACISTS
BEDDING	RATIO
BUS	RD
CREMATE	RERUN
DA	RO
DAD	ROTE
DADDY	ROWS
DANCE	SD
DC	SE
DEBIT	SECRETARY
EARLY	SING
ED	SPEAR
ELATE	TABLET
EM	TADPOLE
EN	TALENT
EO	TB
EPIC	TEACHER
ER	TI
GEAR	TO
HUB	TS
IL	YAWS
IN	UF
IX	WOW
LAND	X-RAY
LEAN	XI
LEE	XXI

THE FINAL WORD

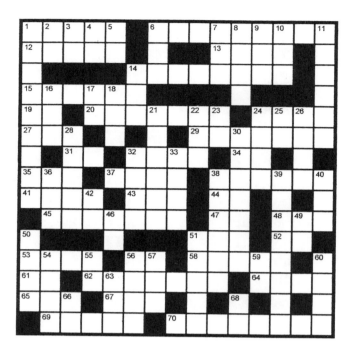

ACROSS

1. Last; end item
6. Opposite of END
12. Not this, but the _____
13. Orderly
14. Take over; be in control
16. President after Roosevelt
19. United Nations
20. Where the bus or train comes in
24. Was
27. At this moment
29. Small, bound sheets of paper
31. Short for HELLO
32. Only; part of a shoe
34. Ancient Egyptian pagan god
35. Adjective meaning a certain one
37. Not there
38. Center

41. European money
43. Environmental Protection Agency
44. First part of UCLA
45. Wander without shape or plan
47. Short for TICKET
48. Observe with the eyes
51. DIAL without the "D"
52. First and third letters of COMMAND
53. Question about time
56. Doctor who delivers babies
58. Expression of contempt
61. Two vowels
62. House; place to live; nest area
64. Country now called Thailand
65. Slang for "YES"
67. Slap; run into
69. Not wrong
70. Not on purpose

DOWN

1. Lucky
2. A thing
3. New Hampshire
4. First two vowels
5. LARGE: abbrev.
6. A scary sound
7. Motel
8. Close by
9. Short for Nathaniel
10. Suffix meaning a follower or believer
11. The dirt we walk on
14. The genetic code in each cell
16. Two random letters
17. Title for a female
18. Machine that gives cash
21. Famous Native American athlete
22. Fifty-five minus fifty-four
23. Opposite of YES
24. Take aim; part of jewelry
25. Last letters of KEEP
26. An English title of nobility
28. Location question
30. Seep slowly
32. What you plant
33. A kind of jet plane
36. Make musical sound without words
38. One whose genes have changed
39. Give the picture in words
40. Organ for seeing
42. Middle of BOAT
46. Northeast
49. Letter before "N"
50 Gone; not here
51. Son of Abraham and Sarah
54. Sixty minutes
55. New Hampshire
56. Short for a death notice
57. A small amount; a piece
59. Letter after "AR"
60. Dirty stuff
63. Open wide and say____
66. Number used to find area of circle
68. Do, Re, ___

WORDS

ACCIDENT	OB
AE	MEANDER
AHH	MI
AO	MIDDLE
ATM	MS
AWAY	MUTANT
BEAD	NAT
BEEN	NE
BEGINNING	NEAR
BIT	NEAT
BOO	NH
CM	NO
DESCRIBE	NOTEPAD
DNA	NOW
DOMINATE	OA
EARL	OB
EM	OBIT
EP	ONE
EPA	OTHER
ES	PI
EURO	RA
EYE	RNO
FINAL	RIGHT
FORTUNATE	SEE
GROUND	SEED
HABITAT	SIAM
HERE	SMUT
HI	SNEER
HIT	SOLE
HOUR	STATION
HUM	TRICKLE
IAL	THE
INN	THORPE
ISAAC	TK
IT	TRUMAN
ITE	UC
LEAR	UN
LG	WHEN
EURO	WHERE
	YUP

YO-YO

ACROSS
1. Art of being without danger
5. Remain; stay
9. Santa Fe is its capitol: abbrev.
11. Humor; wisdom
13. Slow, steady rain
15. Opposite of OUT
16. Magician
18. Short mountain
19. Same as 15 ACROSS
20. Abbrev. for DOWN
22. What we breathe
24. Inquires
26. Really
30. Without danger
31. The Wizard of ___
33. North Dakota
34. Peruvian beasts of burden
35. Crazy, funny
38. Seven in old Rome
40. Short for DOWN
42. A wide shoe width

43. Short for ENCLOSED
44. Half of a toy
46. A metal
48. Part of the heredity helix
50. First letters of HUMAN
51. Place; a matched group
53. A famous African tribe
55. Furniture to sleep on
57. Beginning of XEROX
58. Crippled
59. Overwhelm
61. Slightly open
62. Repeated sound
66. A medical doctor's degree
67. Crawling, stinging insect
70. Two in Roman numerals
71. Silently crawl
73. Beginning of say
74. Stripped horse-like animal
75. Park for animals
76. Close; go fast

DOWN

1. Travel through water
2. Improper contraction
3. Short for FOOT
4. Use your head
6. Opposite of subtract
7. Beginning of IRRIGATION
8. Fasten with a knot
9. National League
10. Happy
12. Opposite of 10 DOWN
14. Energy
16. Knowing; intelligent
17. Same as 48 ACROSS
21. He, she or ___
23. First two letters of ILL
24. One of the seven continents
25. Traded for money
27. Name for Russian king
28. United Nations
29. Kind of ax
30. Three or so
32. Same as 35 ACROSS
36. Northeast
37. Not today or tomorrow
39. Motel; hotel
41. Fifty minus forty-five
45. Exclamation of surprise
47. First and last of CENTS
49. Short for ALFRED
52. Tests
53. Last letter of the alphabet
54. Spaceship
55. Exist
56. Irish for DAD
60. 17 times 0
63. Central Intelligence Agency
64. Short hello
65. Arabic hat
67. First and last letters
68. Northeast
69. Short for tuberculosis
71. Colorado
72. Number used in circles

	WORDS
ACTUALLY	MD
ADD	MT
ADZ	ND
AFRICA	NE
AINT	NL
AIR	NM
JAR	OH
AL	OZ
ANT	PI
ASKS	RNA
AZ	SA
BE	SAD
BED	SAFETY
CIA	SAFE
CO	SET
CREEP	SEVERAL
CS	SOLD
CZAR	SWIM
DA	TB
DN	THINK
DRIZZLE	TIE
ECHO	UFO
EE	UN
ENC	VII
EXAMS	WAIT
FAZE	WISE
FEZ	WIT
FIVE	WIZARD
FT	XE
HI	YESTERDAY
HU	YO
II	ZANY
IL	ZEAL
IN	ZEBRA
INN	ZEE
IR	ZERO
IT	ZINC
LAME	ZIP
LLAMAS	ZOO
MERRY	ZULU

RAIN

OR

SNOW

?

ACROSS

1. The climate at a certain time
7. Country north of the U.S.
12. Short for irregular
13. Female sheep
14. Old-fashioned woman's name
16. Short for pounds
18. Air conditioning: abbrev.
19. Movement of the sea
21. Prefix for NEW
23. Woman's name; soul in Spanish
25. Master of Ceremonies
27. Line; abbrev.
28. Day in Spanish
30. Line from center of circle to edge
33. Opposite of forest
35. Small valley
36. 3.14...
37. Opposite of stop
38. Not crazy; logical
39. Popular; opposite of cold
40. Short for tuberculosis

43. End of YOUR
44. Excursion; journey
46. Part of a foot
48. "Open wide and say ____"
50. Time just before darkness
51. A long, long time
53. Russian space station
56. Plead
57. Short for Edward
59. Physical Education
60. Evenly; justly
63. Award
65. Opposite of Longitude
67. Helps; assists
69. End of BLUE
70. Prefix meaning AGAIN
71. Short for LONG PLAYING
72. Season after winter
73. Season before winter
74. Help letters

DOWN

1. Season for skiing
2. Emergency Room
3. Dry climate
4. Opposite of HE
5. End of THREW
6. Prefix meaning AGAIN
7. Baby bear
8. Not Applicable
9. The first man
10. Ten years
11. Toward in Spanish and Italian
15. Line around middle of the earth
16. Line reaching from pole to pole
17. Beginning of SAY
20. Mr. Zola's first name
22. THE in Spanish and Italian
24. Tell an untruth
26. Signal or pool stick
29. Short for IRREGULAR
31. Hebrew month
32. Short for Daniel
33. Speck; small mark
34. Short street
36. Pshaw; phooey
38. It's a hot time
39. Short height
41. One who makes cakes and cookies
42. Frozen water
45. Carpet
47. Wished; awaited
49. Handle of a sword
52. Northeast
54. Measurement of smarts
55. A measuring stick
56. Computer measurement
58. Guage; old time phone
61. Battery size
62. Beginning of author's name
63. Rind; natural covering
64. Closes; shuts
66. Beginning of DRAMA
68. Same as 74 ACROSS
69. Opposite of DOWN

WORDS

AA	HT
AC	ICE
ADAM	INCH
ADAR	IRG
ADELE	LATITUDE
AH	LONGITUDE
AIDS	IRR
AL	IQ
ALMA	LBS
ARCH	LI
ARID	LIE
BEG	LN
BAKER	LP
BYTE	MIR
CANADA	MC
CUB	NA
CUE	NE
DALE	NEO
DAN	PE
DECADE	PEEL
DESERT	PI
DIA	POO
DIAL	PRIZE
DOT	RADIUS
DRA	RE
DUSK	RUG
ED	RULER
EL	SA
EMILE	SANE
EON	SOS
EQUALLY	SPRING
EQUATOR	ST
ER	SUMMER
EW	TB
EWE	TIDE
FALL	TOUR
GO	UE
HER	UR
HILT	UP
HIM	WEATHER
HOPED	WINTER
HOT	ZIPS

JUST

DO

IT

ACROSS

1. Say aloud
5. Sense an odor
10. Organ for hearing
13. Used for lubricating
14. Makes a little mad
16. Opposite of FROM
17. Opposite of YOUR
18. Not off
19. Asian holiday
21. See
24. Not lost
27. Misplace
29. Same as 13 DOWN
30. United Kingdom; Areas controlled by England
31. A chewy candy
33. Spanish for SUN
34. ONE in German
36. Toward; same as 16 DOWN
37. Opposite of stop
38. Not crazy; logical

39. Popular; opposite of cold
41. Our planet
46. Two vowels
47. Not he
49. Absorbing knowledge
53. Nordic god
54. Short INTEREST
56. Short BOOM
57. Backwards HI
59. Sick
60. United Nations
61. Half a toy
62. Midday meal
66. Clear liquid for drinking
70. California
71. Catch; curve
73. Ray; diverging
76. Slap; punch
77. Move through water
78. Not run

DOWN

1. Dirt
2. About 3.14...
3. THE in Spanish and Italian
4. Opens a lock
5. Scarier
6. List of foods in a restaurant
7. Wide shoe width
8. Fifty-five in old Rome
9. Allow
11. Toward
12. Sweet-smelling flower
15. One's own being
17. A famous hero's initials
20. Opposite of FINGER
22. A big delivery company
23. Beginning of LIKE
24. Product used to produce energy
25. End of meant
26. A small spot
28. Southeast
32. Not against
33. Behold; use eyes
35. Not applicable: abbrev.
37. Find heaviness amount
42. Residue from fire
43. Greek "R"
44. Asian sauce used in U.S.
45. Beginning of LAZY
48. Number used in circles
49. Abbrev. for light
50. Fold into a circular shape
51. Not YES
52. Contraction for I AM
53. One of the five senses
55. Negative
63. United Nations
64. 204 in old Rome
65. Strong dislike
66. Word of pleased surprise
67. Emergency Room
68. Not cooked
89. Short for until
72. Beginning of osmosis

74. District Attorney
75. Beginning of AKIN
76 Short HELLO

WORDS

AK	LV	
ASH	MENU	
AT	MKL	
BEN	MY	
CA	NA	
CCIV	NE	
CH	NO	
CLEAN	NT	
DA	OIL	
DOT	OOM	
EAR	OOO	
EARTH	ON	
EE	OS	
EI	PEEVES	
EIN	PI	
EL	RADIAL	
ER	RAW	
FOR	REBBE	
FOUND	RHO	
FUEL	ROLL	
HATE	ROSE	
HIT	SE	
HO	SEE	
HOOK	SELF	
HOT	SHE	
IH	SI	
ILL	SMELL	
IM	SOIL	
INT	SOL	
KEY	SPEAK	
LA	SPOOKIER	
LEARNING	SWIM	
LET	TERIYAKI	
LOOK	TET	
LOSE	TOFFEE	
LOVE	TOUCH	UN
LT	THOR	YO
	TIL	WALK
	TO	WATER
	TOE	WEIGH
	UK	WOW

AYE, AYE, SIR!

ACROSS

1. Fun; a kind of bird
5. An animal that lives in a sty
8. A small rodent
12. A red vegetable
14. Without any money or assets
16. Dirt; get dirty
18. Curtain; arrange folds of material
19. Following; adjacent to
20. Not off
23. Put together
25. Male pronoun
26. Negative
27. Short for Edward; swirling of liquid
29. Continent where France is
32. Interested in art and music
34. Organ for hearing
36. Opposite of AREN'T
38. Open wide and say ____
39. Sweet potato
40. Has to; be imperative
41. Pole; forbid
42. Droop
43. Beginning of a long stem
45. Consumed

47. Not Miss or Mrs.
48. Yuck!
49. Abbrev. for irregular
50. Nickname for Margaret
51. Short for SMALL
52. Look over quickly; reproduce an image
53. A battery size
55. What a sheep says
56. Okay
57. Mindfulness
59. Beginning of BACK
60. Abbrev. for FLOOR
61. Two in Rome
62. Two vowels
63. Same as 56 ACROSS
64. Department of Motor Vehicles
65. Short for NEAR
66. An old-fashioned girl's name
69. Two more vowels
70. A very wide shoe size
71. A sailor's YES
72. Go to a function

52

DOWN

2. First two letters of the alphabet
3. One of the Christmas colors
4. A famous frog
6. End of SWIPE
7. Not stop
8. Mister
9. Purpose
10. Short for stocking
11. Partner of NEITHER
13. Late
15. Command; selection in a restaurant
17. 200 pounds
21. He built a boat in the Bible
24. Beginning of DUMB
28. A long time; measurement of time
30. Not smooth
31. Famous saint in Ireland
33. A blood condition
35. Exist
37. Without end; forever
38. As Soon As Possible
39. Same as 39 ACROSS
40. Layer inside the earth
42. A famous woman's first name
44. Name of a period in history
46. Four o'clock in some countries
52. Leave in liquid
54. Tale
55. Heat til rolling
58. Name for a grandma
59. Noah built one
60. Eat; give food to
64. Beginning of detest
67. University of Arizona
68. Light: abbrev.
69. Not out

WORDS

AA	LARK
AB	LT
ADD	LULA
AHH	MAGMA
AM	MOUSE
AO	MR
ARE	MS
ARTY	MUST
ASAP	NANA
ATE	NEXT
ATTEND	NO
ATTENTION	NOAH
AYE	NR
BA	OK
BAA	ON
BAR	ORDER
BEET	PATRICK
BOAT	PEGGY
BOIL	PIG
DE	POOR
DMV	RED
DRAPE	REE
DU	RH NEGATIVE
EAR	ROUGH
EDDY	SAG
EEE	SCAN
EITHER	SM
ERA	SOAK
ETERNAL	SOIL
EUROPE	SOX
FEED	STORY
FL	SUSAN
GO	TARDY
HE	TEATIME
IE	TON
II	UA
IN	UGH
IPE	USE
IRR	YAM
KERMIT	YEARS

ANSWERS

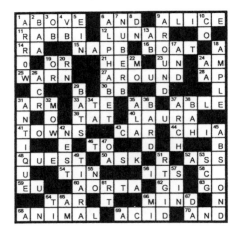

Page 6

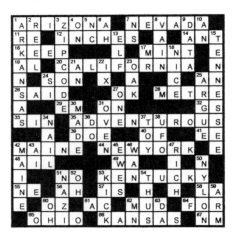

Page 8

Page 10

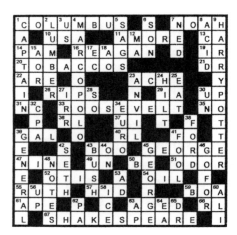

Page 12

Page 14

Page 16

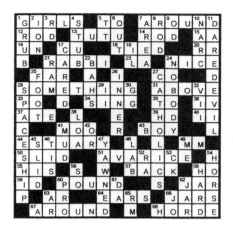

Page 18

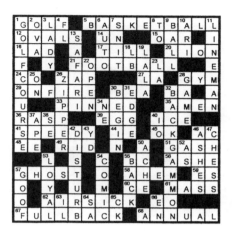

Page 20

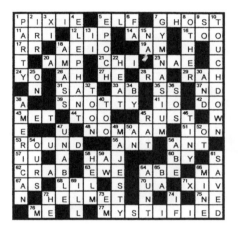

Page 22

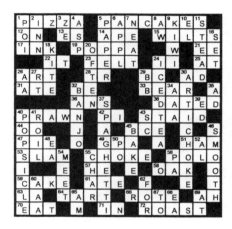

Page 24

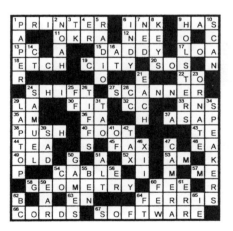

Page 26

Page 28

Page 30

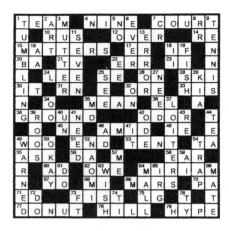

Page 32

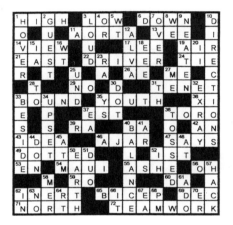

Page 34

Page 36

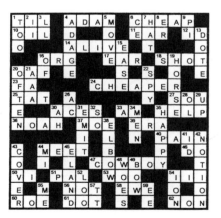

Page 38

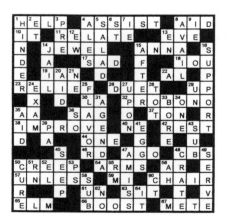

Page 40